Designed by Roxanne Hughes Packham and Hannah Packham
and Frank Boross

Edited by Don Rossi and Elizabeth Lessert

Library of Congress Control Number: 2010902203
ISBN 987-0-9844563-0-7

PUBLISHED 2010
PRINTED IN THE UNITED STATES OF AMERICA

Inspired Design

Roxanne Hughes Packham
and Hannah Packham

Photography by
Mark Lohman

Inspired Design Publications, Inc.
CAMARILLO, CALIFORNIA USA

To my inspiring dad, Bill,
my wonderful husband, Scott,
and my amazing son, Justin.
And Hannah's Papa, Dad,
And Brother

God grant that men of principle shall be our principal men.
— Thomas Jefferson

Inspired Design
CONTENTS

Special Features

Just like you, I am a product of the people I was surrounded with growing up. Grandpa Allan, my dear, larger than life, grandpa was an internationally acclaimed silversmith—and as you will see, he inspired my love for design.

But it was my parents who really inspired me.

My stylish, creative and tenacious mom was there everyday in the carpool line at school, picking us up and chatting about the day. She encouraged both of her daughters to get out of their comfort zones, and she still is an encourager. She is still the one I call if I need a little boost. She and my dad were my biggest fans. But mom is especially amazing in a crisis.

I am in awe of her strength. When my dad was in a near-fatal cycling accident, she rallied the surgical team and got my dad's friends together— no small feat—to pray at the hospital. Mom orchestrated dad's recovery, nursing and the five surgeries that followed. She has weathered other surgeries, and other trials, with amazing fortitude. After 47 years, she and my dad still have a great time together, doing life.

Mom is the most creative person I know. She throws the best dinner parties, gives the best gifts and is the best gift wrapper that ever lived! She throws her heart and soul into her projects for beloved friends and family. It was from her that I learned to do all things with passion and excellence.

Nothing is too good for those mom loves! She hand-paints platters according to the occasion and theme, then color-coordinates them with the wrapping. She always hand makes one of our Christmas gifts. Her love language is gift giving, and her family feels exquisitely loved by the way she attends to details.

I thank God for my mom, yet she is only half of the story. My dad put in endless hours driving me around and saying my prayers with me every night. From an early age, I understood that the love of my heavenly Father must be wonderful, and it was because of how wonderful my earthly father was.

My dad instilled in me a sense of confidence and accomplishment. He was strong and protective. He wrote me notes of encouragement, attended all of my high school track meets and came home for dinner every night, even if he had to go back, as his business was becoming quite successful. I have always known I could do anything I set my mind to, because Dad told me I could—and, of course, he was always right. Dad's determination is legendary, and through his integrity and honesty, I learned what real character looked like.

Dad's work ethic came from his dad, who was a truck driver, and who turned his hard work into a successful trucking company. My dad is honest, ethical, modest and upfront, and it is those qualities that make him a success. He always used to tell me, "You are known for your actions."

I can still hear Dad saying, "A word is like a promise." So, this is my promise to you:

To inspire you to create a home that touches the soul of those within, as well as all who walk through its doors; to share ideas that create beauty, warmth and passion, as I have with hundreds of clients; and to speak from my heart what my family heritage and love of design has taught me.

As women, nurturing our families is the most important job we have. That is why most women I know are always trying to make their home more welcoming, beautiful and enjoyable. Inspired design is a skillful melding of interior design and family tradition, woven together to produce something…well, inspired! This is the gift that I share with my clients.

My clients have graciously allowed me to photograph their homes, and to share the results with you, because they, too, believe that home and family should be celebrated. (Thank you, most lovely and wonderful clients!) It is my hope that the beautiful photographs will inspire spectacular design ideas for your home. Treasured quotes and scripture will help complete the story these photographs tell about how design, and more powerfully, the process of design, can transform homes and the people who live in or visit them. You will also read special observations by my daughter, Hannah. They are included because inspired design is a legacy, and it is meant to be passed from each generation to the next.

Design without a purpose means little to us. Hannah and I wrote this book because we want to celebrate the beauty of the family and the family home. Our purpose is to motivate you to set your table with passion, to invite more people over for dinner, and to do so more often. May this book lead you to host more birthday celebrations, and to just celebrate the beauty of your friends and family!

The beautiful American family—lovely, kind, hardworking, diligent and talented—that is the family we celebrate, and it is yours! In these beautiful homes, on these welcoming tables and in these cozy chairs and charming nooks, we will show you hundreds of ways to make your home more beautiful. You will see combinations of fabrics and how fabric can transform a room; how well placed accessories can bring a room to life; and how, by pleasing the five senses, you can make a beautiful home. You will discover new ideas and combinations to try. But most of all, you will learn that your home matters for eternity.

Do not underestimate the power of your home, nor its ability to change lives. Do not underestimate the power of one tiny, seemingly insignificant, act of kindness. A welcoming smile, a cup of hot tea and an hour in a cozy nook spent listening to a friend can be life-altering. Sending well-loved, cared-for children into the world to contribute to our society in positive, meaningful ways is one of, if not the most significant contributions you will ever make, and your home is a significant part of this endeavor.

Don't for one minute think that your lack of or excess of resources has anything to do with your contribution to the beauty of this world. You never know how someone will be touched by the little things you do—and by the little ways you make your home more inviting. Possessions and pretensions have nothing to do with it! Your willingness and action do. ✑

llan Adler, my beloved grandfather, was a world-renowned silversmith. He was proclaimed a California "Living Treasure" by the Smithsonian Institute. His work is featured on permanent collection at the Smithsonian, the Los Angeles County Museum of Art and at the Huntington Library and Gardens. His jewelry and flatware have been sold at Neiman Marcus, Geary's, Gump's, Ralph Lauren Private Label, and in his own once-famous shop on the Sunset Strip, in Hollywood, California.

Widely known as "the silversmith to the stars," Grandpa Allan was commissioned by Hollywood icons such as Katherine Hepburn and Carol Channing, and leading men including Paul Newman, Cary Grant, Montgomery Clift, Jimmy Gleason and Frank Sinatra. He created the silver logo used on the Sonny & Cher Show, and created items for Michael Jackson. Yet he was a warm, kind and engaging man who made every visitor feel welcomed in his home.

When I was a girl, he and my Grandma Becca, a former Miss Burbank who always had a smile on her face, would regale me with stories. They told me of being commissioned to create the first Miss America and Miss Universe Crowns—and of special creations crafted for Presidents Ford, Nixon and Reagan. Going to their house for dinner and watching them set the table was what inspired me to begin, design and ultimately to write about and photograph the beautiful tables in this book.

away by detail...simplify, simplify. — *Henry David Thoreau*

As a young man, my grandfather was all set to become a building contractor. But his plans changed when he met my grandmother. Her father was seventh-generation silversmith Porter Blanchard (1886-1973), to whom Grandpa Allan soon became apprenticed. Porter Blanchard had learned the trade from his father, George Porter Blanchard, a Colonial Revivalist Silversmith and prominent member of the Society of Arts and Crafts, Boston.

After moving west to California in 1923, Great-Grandpa Porter was instrumental in founding the Arts and Crafts Society of Southern California.

Porter's philosophy was simple. He defined craft as "that thing in industry which is good and beautiful and worth doing for its own sake as well as the money made from it." He said that a craftsman was "a man who has been trained in the practice of some craft with a 'home influence' of love, honor and respect." His favorite expression, "With my hands alone," showed the pride he took in his work. Perhaps his best-known creation was the stunning Commonwealth Coffee Set and Commonwealth flatware (circa 1930), commissioned by actress Anne Harding.

Great-Grandpa Porter's work was carried at Gump's Department stores and fine boutiques across the country. His craftsmanship has been exhibited since 1937 at the Metropolitan Museum of Art, and later that same year, it was celebrated in Paris. More recently, his creations have been displayed at the Los Angeles County Museum of Art, Huntington Library and Gardens

In character, in manner, in style, in all things, the supreme excellence is simplicity.

— Henry Wadsworth Longfellow

and the Smithsonian. His celebrity clients included Harding, Joan Bennett, George Brent, Cary Grant and George Dix. He often referred to Joan Crawford—for whom he created the "Georgian"— as his best customer and friend. But my great-grandfather's greatest legacy was the one he left for his family.

That legacy was passed on to me through my grandparents, and what a legacy it is. You will see it in these pages. Perhaps, one day, you will see something like it in your home. ■ ■ ■

Neither a lofty degree of intelligence nor imagination nor both together go to the making of genius. Love, love, love that is the soul of genius. —Wolfgang Mozart

MISS UNIVERSE PAGEANT -- LONG BEACH, CALIFORNIA -- 1953

MISS UNIVERSE PAGEANT -- LONG BEACH, CALIFORNIA -- 1953

Less is more.
— Robert Browning

Hannah's
POINT OF VIEW

I was born into a family that loves design. That being the case, there was never an undecorated table, or corner, in the house. Every inch of our home was uniquely and beautifully decorated. Not ever cluttered— only beautiful. Whenever there was a party, the table looked gorgeous and clean just like the rest of the house, and I learned something new from helping with the set-up for each event or family get-together. The most amazing highlights from growing up with this creativity were the experiences in themselves, the holiday décor, and the inspiration that I received.

I can remember helping my mom, grandma and great-grandma get ready for parties and get-togethers. Every time I helped out, I learned something exciting that would make a setting look nicer or make the food taste better. I've shared many of those lessons in this book. I can remember putting the forks on the table and folding the napkins; these little experiences helped me to get to know my family, our traditions, and how to make people feel welcome. I also remember loving every single minute of getting to help set-up for something wonderful and, in my eyes, "grown up." At a young age, I got to see how much people appreciate it when you put time into creating the right atmosphere. I speak to all mother figures who read this: It really does make a difference when you teach your children how to make a lovely home.

A word aptly spoken is like ap

...les of gold in settings of silver.

– Proverbs 25:11

I came to absolutely love different decorations for different seasons and holidays, although I didn't realize how much until one year when I was well into middle school. We had our house remodeled, so that year we couldn't easily decorate for Thanksgiving or Christmas. I was so disappointed!

It just didn't seem like Christmas with no trees, garland or festive tables. Not that Christmas is about the decoration, because it isn't; but it definitely does make the atmosphere more festive and enjoyable to have decorations. Even when you don't think so, children do recognize the wonderful holiday atmosphere, and not only because of the presents they will receive on Christmas morning. Children really love the unique feeling of the season that they only get to experience once in awhile. That's certainly why I loved it, and why I still do. Simple traditions do not go unnoticed. The feeling you get during each holiday should in some way be magical, and décor contributes greatly to a unique and magical feeling.

Even as a child, I saw how much my family loved what they did, and I think that seeing the passion in my family helped to engrave into my mind that a love for what you do is essential to be successful. When you find what you love, life is more enjoyable, and you have an outlet when you need it. I now love design—particularly costume design. I now try to practice sketching as much as I can, and when I do I love it! I know that growing up with a family that encouraged me in this way has helped me to find what I love. And I will forever be grateful.

– Hannah

ALLAN

ALLAN & HANNAH

DAD & ROXANNE

SCOTT, BILL & ELIOT   PORTER & ROXANNE & BILL   THE SHAWNEE & ALLAN, BECCA & HANNAH   THE SHAWNEE

THE MEN OF THE FAMILY

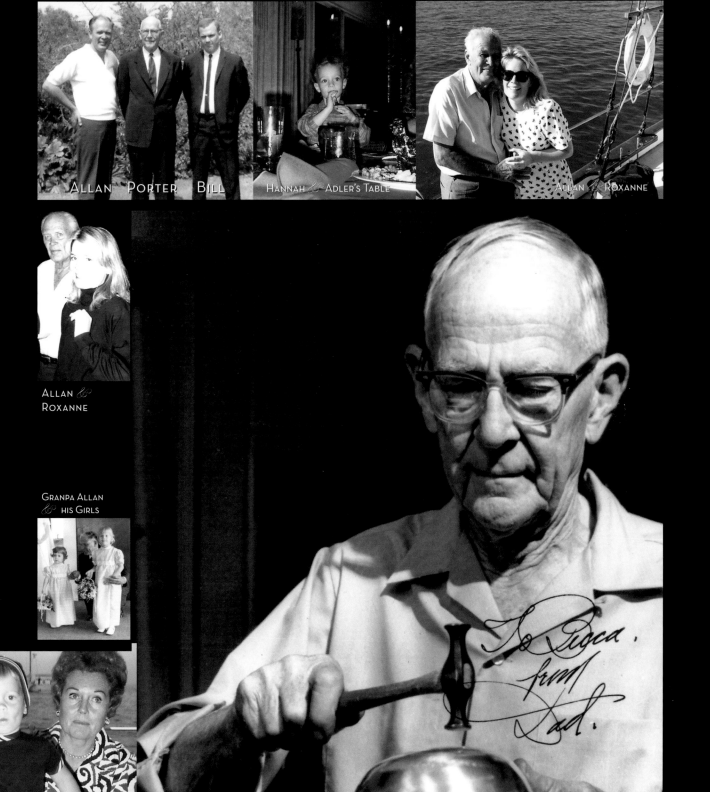

ALLAN PORTER BILL

HANNAH & ADLER'S TABLE

ALLAN & ROXANNE

ALLAN &
ROXANNE

GRANPA ALLAN
& HIS GIRLS

BILL ROXANNE & BECCA

Beautiful Heart, Beautiful Home

"Our deepest fear is not that we are inadequate. Our deepest fear is that we are powerful beyond measure. It is our light, not our darkness, that most frightens us. We ask ourselves, who am I to be brilliant, gorgeous, talented, and fabulous? Actually, who are you not to be? You are a child of God. Your playing small doesn't serve the world. There's nothing enlightened about shrinking so that other people won't feel insecure around you. We are all meant to shine, as children do. We are born to make manifest the glory of God that is within us. It's not just in some of us, it's in everyone. And as we let our own light shine, we unconsciously give other people permission to do the same. As we are liberated from our own fear, our presence automatically liberates others."

—Marianne Williamson

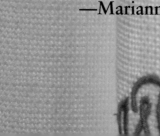

eautiful, as used throughout this book, does not mean simply external beauty. There are hundreds of excellent interior design books that illustrate and discuss beauty for beauty sake. (Ask my husband. He says I have them all!) When we speak of beauty, we cannot separate external beauty from the internal beauty that radiates from the heart—or in this case, the heart of the home. Words like beautiful, stylish, elegant, classic and timeless conjure up images of people whose presence is hard to forget. You cannot have a classically beautiful home, or be a classy, beautiful person, without true inner beauty: warmth, kindness, and empathy.

True beauty also stimulates the five senses. A beautiful home—indescribably warm and visually stimulating—envelops you in coziness and love! Touching all of the five senses sends the message that you have eagerly awaited your guests' arrival, and that they are truly welcome in your home. Think of your guests as honorees. Think of the five senses as five ways to envelop them in warmth.

Touch

Touch can be literal and figurative in entertaining. An embrace or pat on the back upon entering conveys a sense of intimacy. Being greeted at the door with a welcoming touch is much more important than finishing up the cooking, lighting candles or setting the table. If you must finish something else, greet the guests first. Then finish up! If you are entertaining a business associate or a new acquaintance, a handshake or pat on the shoulder will do quite well. But you will also touch your guests figuratively throughout the evening. Soft upholstery, comfy pillows or cashmere blankets make sitting on a couch so much more pleasant. Soft is key.

Smell

A fragrant candle, a simmering pot of cider on the stove or a plate of freshly baked cookies make a wonderful entrance to a home. A few votives lit and placed around the front door, with some fresh seasonal greens or flowers, rarely goes unnoticed. Fresh flowers in your window boxes, or pots outside, are also very welcoming. Realtors comment frequently that the smell of freshly baked bread or cookies helps a home to sell! That is a strong statement of the message that is sent when your home smells pleasant. Seasonal scents bring the outdoors in, and a few pine boughs, for example, are simple to cut and bring indoors. You can place them in a vase of water, across the mantle or even inside the fireplace.

Sight

Obviously, a clean and tidy house is, in general, more appealing than a dirty one. But hospitality will compensate for a less than perfect home. This can be as simple as a sign with a welcoming quote or verse that lets your guests know you are excited to see them. But sight also includes the mood of the room.

A room lit completely by candlelight, with a soft fire in the fireplace, conveys a deep sense of warmth. Nothing is more elegant than candlelight, and as a bonus, it helps conserve electricity. Lighting a room with candles is also romantic and soft. I never feel completely ready to entertain until all the candles are lit. The glow candles cast creates a delicate, shadowy, warm and appealing look. It hides a multitude of flaws, including dust, a slightly dirty floor or crayon marks, and everyone looks more attractive in candlelight.

Another way to make your home more visually appealing to your guests' sense of sight is with place cards, menus, and flowers thoughtfully arranged. As guests come to the table they will see these touches and know that time and care were taken in anticipation of their arrival.

Thoughtfulness is key. A hand-cut arrangement of flowers is just as thoughtful, perhaps more so, than a store bought arrangement. My friend Wendy cuts roses from her garden and puts them in a jelly jar. It just warms my heart that she took those fifteen minutes out of her busy day to do something nice for me when I visit.

Sound

Appeal to your guests' sense of sound with subtle classical, jazz, or soft contemporary music playing in the background. Classical music, in particular, can be quite soothing. Medical studies show that it raises natural serotonin levels in the brain and helps children retain what they study. Now, I am not a doctor, but I do know that music is soothing, and certainly can't hurt!

What you say also counts when it comes to filling your home with pleasing sounds; so fill your home with encouraging words and uplifting speech. A cheerful greeting and a compliment upon entering will lift your guests' spirits. I wouldn't suggest making something up, but you can always find something nice to say to a friend or a guest.

Taste

Taste, of course, means food. Since there are thousands of delicious recipes out there I am not including any recipes, but if you aren't a gourmet chef, don't worry! Keep it simple. Sometimes an intricate and complicated meal can require so much time in the kitchen that you won't be able to welcome or mix with your guests. It is just possible if you are never ready when your guests arrive, you need to prepare simpler recipes and lower your expectations. You can always hire someone to serve, if it's important to cook in gourmet style.

Have some candies and nuts in dishes throughout the main area, just in case the meal is a little later than hoped for. But elaborate meals are not necessary to make guests feel welcomed and loved; it is better to be relaxed. Do remember to ask about food allergies and accommodate friends who are vegetarians or vegans. You will be showing your thoughtfulness, and they will feel more welcomed.

Little things can make a big difference. I know they have for me. I have a friend named Susan, for instance, who each year bakes a cake for our birthdays that incorporates favorite things like colors, sports team, pastimes and the like. It is such a thoughtful touch. My friend and neighbor, Sharyl, is the best cook, but what sets her apart is the way that she makes everyone feel comfortable and relaxed in her home. She has candles lit, and there are always flowers or something fun on the table!

My friend, Joy, brought homemade scones and hot tea to my car door when I gave her son a ride to school. A bowl of chicken soup, from Susan, a basketful of snacks, from Suzanne, and a beautiful fresh basket of flowers, from Tamma, were treats when I had sinus surgery.

It's all about thoughtfulness. So while you are preparing to enjoy your home with guests, or alone, mentally check if all the five senses have been covered: touch, sound, feel, taste and sight. Add a little kindness, and you will have the perfect recipe for the perfect time.

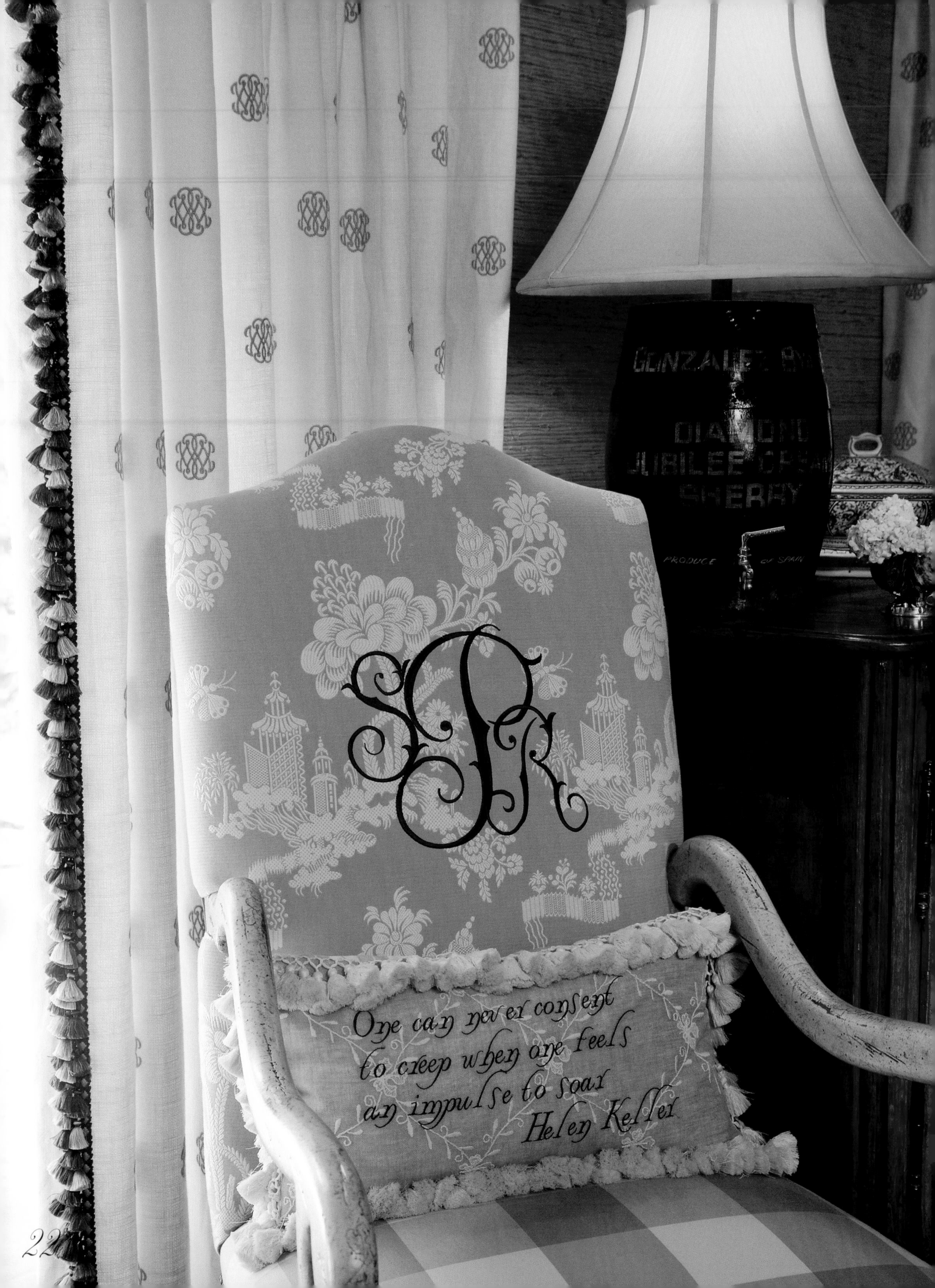

One can never consent
to creep when one feels
an impulse to soar
Helen Keller

Hannah's POINT OF VIEW

Pretty much everything I know about hospitality, I learned from Mom.
I learned how to be myself. Mom helped me grow to love design— not by pushing me to love it, but letting me slowly grow to appreciate it all on my own. My family has inspired me to love design because they all are so talented. I grew up wanting to be like them. I would love to carry on the tradition and create inspired designs, just like my family has done.

—Hannah

Decorating Well:
Some Practical Advice

Designing and decorating a home is not an overnight project. It is a process that can most clearly be described as textured layering. Once the physical structure of a home is complete (a process that would require a book of its own), the layering of decorating begins. You start by selecting the treatment or color for the ceiling and walls; flooring and rugs; drapery and window coverings; lighting—both fixed and free standing; furniture—including case goods and upholstery; and finally, the accessories.

Keep in mind that while there are several places you should not skimp because it will show, you don't necessarily have to spend your entire savings to get a beautiful home. You do have to be selective. Don't try to do everything all at once. There are very few people who can do that—both for financial and sanity reasons. If you spend a little more than you wanted on drapes, wait until the following year to do the wall covering. You will be better off investing in something long-lasting and high quality—even if it takes five years to complete—than filling your home with cheap furniture, and drapes and treatments that will be worn out and look terrible in a few years. Don't be in a rush to get things done. Layering takes time.

Walls and ceilings are a key element; they dominate by their size alone. A color that fits the mood and spirit of the room is vital. Whether it is dark and bold or soft and luscious, make sure you love the way a room feels once it is painted. Don't worry about a dark color making a room feel small. Think warm and cozy instead—and thus, more intimate. The bottom line on color is, if you love it, do it!

Texture in a home, and especially on the walls, adds tremendous sophistication and warmth. Grass cloth, ultra suede, silk and linen are all beautiful, but there are a few basic principles you should observe.

"The beginning is the most important part of work."

— Plato

25

In a powder room or a bathroom without a moisture issue, upholstering the walls is a dramatic way to make a little space with four walls and porcelain look amazing and unique. Grass cloth is always my favorite for whipping a room together, but especially if my client only wants to do just one or two things to a room to give it a facelift. Nothing pulls a room together more than a beautiful grass cloth texture, with a collection of photographs, beautiful prints or stunning art. It takes a little color from the collections or fabrics and disperses it throughout the room. It can be the focal point if you choose a periwinkle, turquoise or brightly colored toile or floral with all-white furniture, drapery and bedding. It makes the whole look complete.

Flooring is so important because it gives an immediate design flavor upon entering a home. Dark Spanish pavers convey a warm, relaxed, European style. Dark hardwoods inspire traditional design. While both can be made formal or casual, they each have a very distinct flavor. Carpet is always nice in bedrooms because it is soft and not so cold on the feet when getting out of bed, but it is never my preference for an entire house, because in a well-used house with lots of traffic, it looks too worn out, too fast. A hard-surfaced floor is usually far more durable than carpet. It is the floor; it does take a beating and no flooring is without a few pitfalls.

Beautiful fabrics are critical to beautiful drapes. This is one place where cutting costs always shows. I joke with my clients that I can always do less expensive drapery; they just have to choose the less expensive fabric, which never happens, because you can tell the difference. If you

I tell you, the more I think, the more I feel that there is nothing more truly artistic than to love people. – Vincent VanGogh

27

In art there is a feeling of harmony which underlies all endeavors. There is no true greatness in art or science without that sense of harmony. - Albert Einstein

have a smaller budget than you'd like, linen is the very best choice for elegant but not-fussy drapery; however, if you don't like wrinkles, linen is not for you. I cannot stand the look of polyester drapes; so if cost is an issue, use an inexpensive silk or linen. Just remember that silk is very susceptible to sun damage, so make sure it is lined well and not in a spot that gets harsh direct sun.

The old adage, "You get what you pay for," is especially true with upholstered furniture. I use only high-end companies for my clients, because upholstery looks cheap if it is made cheaply. Fabric selection is equally as important on furniture as it is in drapery, it must fit the utility of the piece. If it is for a sofa in the family room, you want a strong, durable fabric, and if you have kids, you will probably want a pattern to hide spills. You can use silks on living room furniture that is not in the way of direct sun, if you like a more formal look. Linen is beautiful and relaxed in slipcovers, if they aren't made to look sloppy. If that's the case, they will just look sloppier with time! Tailored slipcovers are the best, because they can be dry

*In our life there is a single color,
as on an artist's palatte, which
provides the meaning of life
and art. It is the color of love.*

— *Marc Chagall*

cleaned or remade in another fabric, if you tire of the fabric after it is worn. The arms of a sofa are key to a beautiful, classic room. I love the English arm because you can curl up and snuggle to watch television or read a book, and it looks very elegant when not in use.

Accessories are the most important part of the design process, because if everything else is done well, and the accessories are done wrong, the entire design will fall flat. The wrong scale is the main culprit, but buying too cheaply is another. In the beginning of my design business, I had many clients who felt they couldn't spend any more money and told me their home felt "finished," but the design wasn't finished! Sometimes just a spot of color or a different texture changes the whole feeling and makes it come together.

Now, in my initial presentation to my clients, I always include a portion of the budget simply marked "accessories." That way once the furniture is selected, I can find the best lamps, vases, clocks, bowls, coffee table books, fireplace screens, etc. And because I have allowed

Hannah's
POINT OF VIEW

One benefit of a well decorated home is that it makes your company feel welcome. Your guests will feel like you spent time to make them feel at home, peaceful and welcomed. Feeling welcomed tends to be a good feeling; I think we can all agree on that. So by spending time on your home, you can make your friends feel valued during their stay in your home.

— Hannah

that in the budget, my clients know this is an integral part of the design. To me, to forget accessories in your home is like forgetting to wear your shoes when you go out!

Throughout the beautiful teal and khaki home I photographed for this chapter is an alluring art collection that my clients, Bill and Janet, had collected over approximately 20 years. We were able to pull the subtle colors out of the art into the room through the medium-hued khaki carpet, the teal grass cloth in the master and sitting room and the beige and khaki grass cloth in the dining room. Although the physical house remained untouched, it wasn't until we darkened the carpets, covered the walls and put breathtaking fabrics into the window treatments that the artwork began to sing. Much of the furniture stayed the same. We re-upholstered a very comfy sofa in the family room and some treasured family bergere chairs in the living room, kept the exquisite dining table, but toned the gold down on the details with a favorite refinisher of mine. The fabrics we chose were the key to making this design take flight. The floral we used in the kitchen nook, combined with the teal sheers on the windows look stunning with the pool outside peeking through. The use of layering in this home was key, and thankfully, the art that inspired the color scheme was soft and enchanting, while also very dramatic. ■ ■ ■

If you judge people you have no time to love them.

— *Mother Teresa*

Uniquely You

Uniquely You

Just as you were masterfully created, unique like no other, your home should be unique! Not only should your family history be represented in some way, but your true loves—people, places and things—should be reflected in your home. If they are, your home will be enchanting, beautiful, distinctive, and unrepeatable.

Classic, original beauty in a home is a combination of several things: beautiful fabrics, timeless case goods (hardwood furniture), classic upholstery (English arm sofas, bergere chairs, lovely sofas), treasured family antiques and exquisite artwork. Attractive and eclectic pieces make a home one-of-a-kind. These include new and inherited items—handmade treasures crafted by children and friends, sentimental collections, china, silver, and historic family photographs in silver frames. When walking through the different rooms in your home, you should smile because each object reminds you of a trip, a dear friend, or a special time.

Personally, and in our homes, we are comprised of parts that make us both extraordinary and ordinary, and honestly, in need of improvement. Emphasize the extraordinary, the unique, and the positive!

My client turned dear friend, Karen Armstrong, whose home is the main home photographed for this chapter, told me on our first meeting that she was very hesitant to use an interior designer because she'd had an unpleasant experience with another designer who had taken over and imposed her style on Karen. That is the last thing most women want, and more than anything, Karen wanted her house to be a unique reflection of her family and her "favorite things."

Karen is a very stylish dresser. Her unique collection of ruffled skirts, shoes with exquisite flowers or detail, unique necklaces with handcrafted flowers, buttons and such reflect

Remember always that you have not only the right to be an individual, you have an obligation to be one. — Eleanor Roosevelt

her delightful, graceful taste. Naturally beautiful, she typically wears no makeup, and is definitely a no-fuss, no-muss person. Having three very young children, she doesn't want high-maintenance anything. This was my starting point! After walking through her home and taking stock of her collections (scouring her closets!!), listening to her wishes, her priorities in design and life and observing, I came to the design that we completed a few months later. You can do the same: take the cues from what you love and are passionate about.

Here are a few highlights from Karen's inspired design:

After seeing her MacKenzie-Childs plate and serving piece collection, for which I also have a passion, I decided that these pieces would become a central part of her decor. Karen also showed me her antique and new cake plate collection, complete with a wonderful assortment of faux cakes and pies, and beautiful domes. This became the main theme of the kitchen. We also mixed a few pieces into other rooms as lamps and candy dishes, to carry the feeling throughout the main floor.

I listened carefully as Karen told me that she didn't just want a fun, whimsical home. She said she wanted warmth, elegance and serenity. With her love for MacKenzie-Childs pottery, which is bold, full of color and patterns, I had my work cut out for me.

We carefully selected light, warm wood to soften the look of that pottery, while adding a classic, silk, black and white gingham check in the dining room to pull the feeling of the room toward traditional design. We used a cheerful, kelly green toile in the sitting room, dining room and in the long entry hall. We added a classic, sunny, uplifting fabric that was still traditional but a perfect complement to the pottery and the cake plates.

In the family room where her three young children played, roughhoused, colored and did messy crafts, my job was to create a graceful and cozy room that would stand up to heavy use and look just as good in five years as it did on the day I finished. To accomplish this we used a combination of busy, colorful florals, stripes, toiles, and plaids to hide dirt; cotton fibers that could easily be washed; and sturdy, well-built and upholstered furniture.

The coffee table we selected was dark, classic mahogany-stained wood. We also chose a lovely, classic round table for a whimsical MacKenzie-Childs lamp. A beautiful, hand-painted floor/rug art that Karen found while visiting her hometown in Texas was placed under an existing antique pine table, which we set for this book with MacKenzie-Childs collection. As a finishing touch, we incorporated a treasured blanket, given to Karen's husband by a grateful patient, knowing that her house wouldn't really be a home until all their treasured heirlooms had been thoughtfully incorporated into the design. ■ ■ ■

Hannah's
POINT OF VIEW

It is important to be yourself, because there is only one you. You can do great things that no one else can do. You can say things that no one else can say. You can think things that no one else can think. If you think that what you do won't make a difference, you are wrong. You can make a difference. Being yourself also speaks to other people and inspires them to be unique, too. Seriously, when you are true to yourself, you will do the world more good.

— Hannah

You have it *easily in your power* to increase the sum total of this world's happiness now. How? By giving a few words of *sincere appreciation* to someone who is

lonely or discouraged. Perhaps you will forget tomorrow *the kind words you say today*, but the recipient may cherish them over a lifetime. — DALE CARNEGIE

41

Character contributes to beauty. It fortifies a woman as her
discipline, fortitude, and integrity can do a great deal

...outh fades. A mode of conduct, a standard of courage, ...to make a woman beautiful. — Jacqueline Bisset

43

I was not born to be forced. I will breathe after my
nature, it dies; and so a

own fashion... If a plant cannot live according to his

nan. —Henry David Thoreau

45

Be yourself.
The world worships the original.
— Ingrid Bergman

57

"For *Attractive* lips, speak words of kindness. For *Lovely* eyes, seek out the good in people. For a *Slim* figure, share your food with the hungry. For *Beautiful* hair, let a child run his fingers through it once a day. For *Poise*, walk with the knowledge that you'll never walk alone. People, more than things, have to be restored, renewed, revived, reclaimed, and redeemed; *Never* throw out anybody. Remember, if you ever need a helping hand, you will find one at the end of each of your arms. As you grow older, you will discover that you have two hands, one for helping yourself and the other for helping others."

— *Sam Levenson,*

spoken by Audrey Hepburn

48

A cheerful look brings joy to the heart, and good news gives health to the bones. — Proverbs 15:30

49

51

The Adler's Table

One of the greatest lessons my grandfather taught me is that a beautiful table is at the heart of inspired design. It is where deeper relationships are formed through conversation, and in my grandparents' home it was the center of the action. Their charm and genuine warmth added the exclamation mark that made a dinner at their house a memory to be treasured. No wonder our family still focuses on a beautifully set table for a celebration of any sort.

Grandpa would often say, "A beautiful table is something over scale with something simple. Simplicity is to me beautiful design. A fabulous table is a beautiful wood table with large, oversize plates, beautiful silver, fabulous stemware, with water glasses perhaps twice the size of normal. I like a bare table to show off the simplicity of the combination of flatware, plates and stemware...the whole ensemble. No placemats, no tablecloth."

"I love natural materials snuggled up next to each other," he told me, "especially the different textures. But simplicity to me also means clean lines. If using straight lines use straight. If using curvy lines use curvy. It's all in the purity of design. Don't mix. Like a good painting, good design is knowing when to stop. A good designer knows when to put the brush down. In other words, he knows when to quit."

When I asked him about the most beautiful table he could remember, he recalled a visit with Grandma Becca to the 6th floor of the Los Angeles Times Building. Dorothy Chandler invited them. They were ushered into the executive boardroom, which held a 30-foot long rosewood table. It was set with silver, crystal and china on its bare surface. At its center was a fabulous silver bowl filled with flowers.

"The simplicity of it was breathtaking," Grandpa Allan said, "and it didn't run competition with too much stuff cluttering up the table. I don't like tall centerpieces where you can't see the other people and talk with them. A silver bowl with flowers in the center of the table is lovely."

To Grandpa Allan, every detail was important, including lighting. "Before electricity, you ate by candlelight," he told me, "and I think a room looks best lit by natural candlelight." He showed me an old iron freestanding candlestick he used, and added, "Candles should be used to light the sides of the table, not to distract by lighting from the center. I like the use

of candles and mirrors to create shadows. I like a buffet with simple things. Ornate with simple. Indirect lighting shows off beautifully. I like soft music in the background."

My grandfather was always so honest. "Some people can be very boring to have over, because all they talk about is themselves and they are completely self-involved. We don't usually have them over too often," he said. I asked him, "What interesting people have you had over?" "Well, Stanley Marcus," he replied. When I asked why, he said, "Well, they own Neiman Marcus, isn't that good enough?"

I still remember watching Grandma Becca set the table. From the time I was a very little girl and could barely see over the counter, I would follow her around as she prepared for gatherings. She would fill a bowl or vase, then go outside to a flower bush or tree to cut the greenery. She would walk back into the black tiled kitchen, arrange the flowers just so, then carrying them to the dining table and placing it in just the right spot on the table.

Usually the flower was a simple white gardenia, floating in an Allan Adler silver bowl, gorgeous in its simplicity! Sometimes it was greenery in the tall crystal vase that now adorns my table. Every arrangement looked so majestic and elegant. I can remember it like it was last night.

Grandpa Allan told me that it was Grandma Becca's voice teacher who set the most memorable table he had ever seen. "The plates were oversized, blue and white with an oriental pattern," he said. I told her teacher that when she got rid of them, I would love to have them, that they were beautiful. So she gave them to me."
He proudly showed them to me, and told me he would put them with his Epitomous Swedish Modern flatware, because both look fabulous with wood. After he died, Grandma Becca gave them to me, and I love them. They are photographed in this book. ■ ■ ■

Setting the Table

hether simple and elegant, or filled with bright color and treasured silver heirlooms, a beautifully set table is a work of art that can also touch people's hearts. No doubt you've set plenty of tables, but here are some easy, quick ideas that will make your table look breathtaking.

Begin with the table itself. If you have a beautiful wood or glass table, leave it bare, without a tablecloth. Wood or glass is beautiful to layer, and placemats can add some gorgeous color while still allowing the beauty of the natural wood to show through. The only time I'd consider a tablecloth is to cover a table you don't love the look of—or for a tea party, if you use a lace tablecloth that looks feminine and tea-like.

Use china, porcelain or pottery plates. One of my favorite designs is to set a gorgeous table with white plates and serving pieces. You can add a bit of color with the flowers or linens, but it is so crisp and refreshing to use all white. You can dress up a set of white plates for every holiday and occasion. Often, you can pick up sets rather inexpensively to add to an existing one.

Don't neglect the centerpiece. There are many items you can use, alone or with flowers, to set a gorgeous table—at a moments notice, and with no stress. Hurricane candles and candlesticks are one example. Use them plain, with just a candle, or fill them with seasonally colored items like cranberries, coffee beans or seashells to add a festive touch. Fresh flowers are always beautiful, but so is plain greenery such as lemon branches, boxwood branches, or at Christmas, pine boughs.

Keep a good collection of linen napkins on hand. In the end you will save so much money that you would have spent on paper napkins, and they look so beautiful on a table. Use them freshly pressed, and either folded or pulled through a napkin ring—which is my favorite look, because it can be relaxed and adds a burst of color in contrast to the plates—or next to them. You can also fold napkins loosely into quarters and put them in a wine glass. That adds a pretty pop of fabric, and can coordinate the scheme as well.

Have a good set of flatware. If you can't afford sterling silver flatware, you can often find affordably priced silver plate at an antique store. Because flatware is often thought of as a "thing of the past"—something that young women today don't value—you often find complete sets, still in their felt-covered cases. They may have inches of dust on them, but they are crying out to be used.

Add sparkle to your table with glass. Clean glassware, whether fine crystal or not, adds beauty to your table, and when candles are lit it will sparkle! A glass salad bowl is always so pretty, and it highlights the beauty of the lettuce and colorful vegetables it holds. Silver salad servers look great on top, and silver or glass salt and pepper shakers not only complete the necessities for the table, but also go with any of the choices you make for a typical or fancy night's dinner.

Use place cards and menus to show forethought and sentiment. The menu can have the occasion, and the actual menu printed on it—or just a verse, poem or quote, and the reason for the celebration. I love to assign this task to my daughter as she can fill out the place cards and make the menu while I am making the dinner.

Don't be afraid your life will end; be afraid it will never begin.
—Grace Hansen

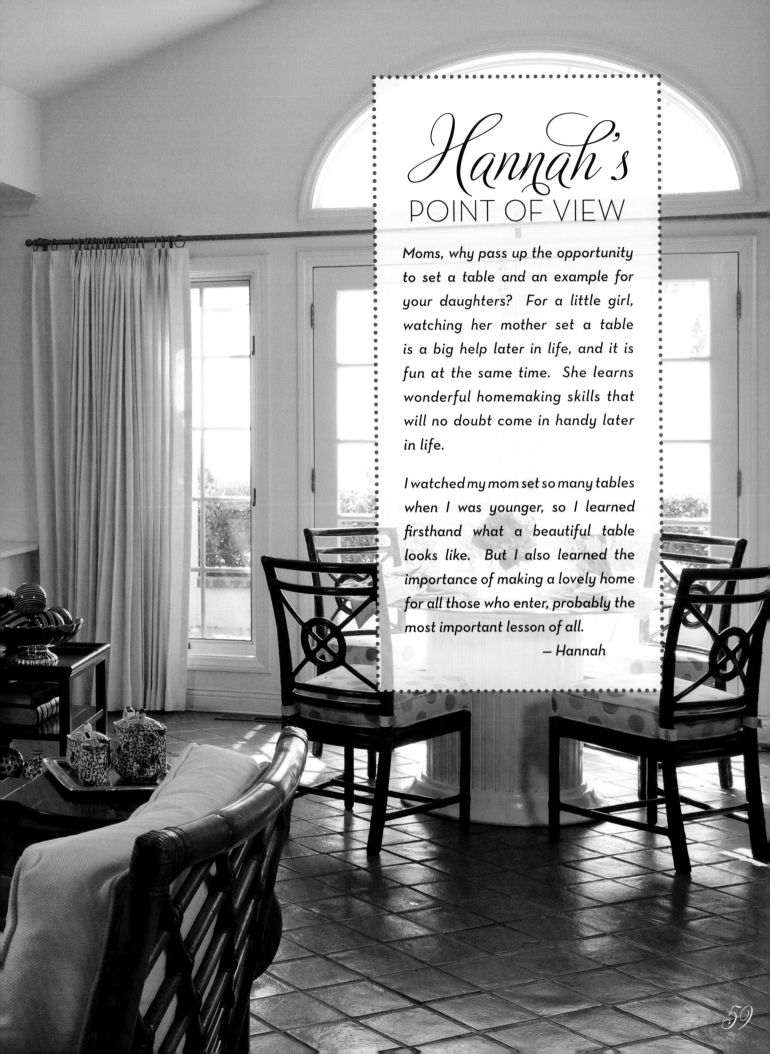

Hannah's
POINT OF VIEW

Moms, why pass up the opportunity to set a table and an example for your daughters? For a little girl, watching her mother set a table is a big help later in life, and it is fun at the same time. She learns wonderful homemaking skills that will no doubt come in handy later in life.

I watched my mom set so many tables when I was younger, so I learned firsthand what a beautiful table looks like. But I also learned the importance of making a lovely home for all those who enter, probably the most important lesson of all.

— Hannah

*We make a living by what we get,
but we make a life by what we give.*
— Norman MacEwan

61

A mother's arms are more comforting than anyone else's — Diana, Princess of Wales

Collections for Entertaining

Part of our home's uniqueness is due to the antiques we purchased while living in Europe. A few months after my husband and I were married, the Navy sent us to Spain for a three-year tour of duty. We traveled all over Europe and bought some fabulous antiques in Portugal, France, Belgium, Germany, Austria and, of course, Spain.

Traveling around Europe was an amazing experience for a newly married 24-year old. While our budget was tiny, I learned how to stretch a dollar and purchase wisely with what we had. I made fewer purchases, but purchased the best quality we could afford. We didn't have a kitchen (or dining room) table for the first three years of marriage, because I refused to buy a cheap table that would not last long. Instead, I saved up for a few years to buy a wrought iron table base in Paris. It still sits in our home, a treasured and favorite piece, almost 20 years later.

I love that table as much now as I did then. It was a great purchase, and a great story. We had to put it in the backseat of our car, which was already filled with glass from Poland. I had to ride for more than 20 hours with my seat tilting forward, so that the table would fit.

I didn't complain because the table was beautiful, and of course, my back didn't hurt because I was so young. But I did learn an important lesson through this and other early experiences: I can't bear to waste money on anything disposable.

That's especially true when it comes to items for a party, such as paper plates, napkins and cups. I began to notice that each time there was an event, I spent at least $40 on paper goods. If I had several events close together, I could end up spending hundreds of dollars with nothing to show for it. So I started borrowing things from friends and investing the savings in something that could be re-used each time I had a party.

I recommend that you do the same. Buy a set of linen napkins, for example, for one party, and borrow someone else's extra glasses, and plates. The next time, buy glasses, borrow the plates, and so on. In not too much time, you will have a collection of nice things that will last for years to come.

Here's another example: We were in Austria for a conference, and I, still on a newlywed's budget, went out with the older wives. We visited the most charming Austrian barn, and I found a wrought iron chandelier that I just loved. There was a problem, however: my budget for the whole trip—for souvenirs and, probably, some meals—was around $200.

Well, I thought myself quite the practical shopper. Instead of squandering a little here and there with nothing to show for it but cheap little throwaway items, I bought something that still hangs in our family room today. I was so proud, but my much-less-proud husband inquired how we were getting this chandelier back to Spain on the airplane. I hadn't even thought about that.

With some duct tape and a sheet from the hotel bed, we finally wrapped the chandelier and carried it on the plane with just one little issue. Of course "we" was Scott, and the "little" issue was a large amount of pleading and begging with the flight attendants. But my collection was on

its way, and over the years I've become very fond of it.

The three main categories for collecting are: the linen closet, the china cupboard (formal and casual) and the tableware trousseau. I also keep some entertaining staples in the pantry, so that I don't have to run to the store if I have to welcome guests on very short notice. These include crackers, nuts and frozen hors d'oeurves.

Clearly, budget plays a part in your collections. But look at your budget as your guidelines for creativity. Having said that, no matter how small your collections are, having a special place for them will make them more special, functional and easy to use. For the linen collection, that place could be the hall closet, or a shelf or two. It might also be a freestanding cabinet or armoire, or the guest room closet.

The Linen Closet

An ideal setting for the linen closet is close to your dining table. This makes setting the table so much more convenient. The linen closet should also be close to the bedrooms, however, because it will also hold sheets and towels.

One very practical and liberating tip before setting up your closets: get rid of superfluous junk—the stuff you never use, don't like and isn't sentimental. It may be someone else's idea of gorgeous, useful or whatever, but, in your home, it just sits on a shelf, accumulating dust. You never use it. If your children used it to set the table, you'd be horrified.

Keep everything in your closets/armoires in good or nearly perfect condition, so that it's easy to go to the closet, select, and set the table. Who needs seven tablecloths, if three are old and you would never use them? Some of my clients like to take older or infrequently used items to a consignment store and use the money they get for them for the next set. Some donate to their favorite thrift store, and others trade with each other! Once the unused items are gone, take care of what is left. Finely pressed, fresh smelling linens are so much more fun to choose from when setting the table. Scents like lemon or grapefruit are wonderful.

There are hundreds of books on organizing linens. I like to arrange them with the most used as the most accessible, then by color, and then, perhaps, by holiday. No matter where you store your linens, make sure they are easily accessible and seen, so you can open the cabinet door, look and select. That way, setting the table is

quicker and easier, and you will probably set it more often. A neatly kept linen closet is like your own little store, easy to get to, and easy to select from. The ritual of getting ready is so much more fun when it's organized, and thus free from stress.

The China Cupboard

The China Cupboard is your most important cabinet, because it is typically the one that gets used the most. It must contain the basics: plates, silverware and glass, cups and teacups.

I love beautiful plates! They are the key component of the China cabinet, a critical part of your entertaining collection, and arguably, the most practical and versatile. A large plate collection ensures that when entertaining large groups, you don't have to resort to paper, rent or borrow, so it saves money. But equally or more important, it saves time. The more easily you can prepare for entertaining, the more stress-free your meals, dinners and parties will be.

In addition to their obvious use, plates make wonderful design easy. Throughout the home, plates can play a major role. You can make lovely visual statements by hanging them in unique combinations and patterns on your walls, and that's a great way to store them as well. Plates also look stunning when arranged carefully on an armoire or buffet.

Stacked interestingly on bookshelves, plates can be useful as bookends, and they provide great storage as well. They can be arranged around doors as a "frame," or hung in a vertical line in a small wall space for an attractive decorative element. Plates can be placed on a stand on top of a stack of books. Plates can be the accessories on a buffet or entry table. Under a candle, plates can be striking, while protecting the furniture and acting as a shield against hot wax. Their uses are almost endless.

Practically speaking, a white plate collection is the best! You can add different types, styles and sizes as you go, or buy the same brand and "pattern," but white never goes out of style. My "white" collection consists of plates, bowls and serving pieces of all size and shapes, and I love their versatility. Whatever the season or celebration, I can work around white plates, using them as a base and making a striking table setting.

A white table is the most elegant table that can be created. I often use white plates, crisp white napkins and flatware. To these,

I simply add candles and some beautiful glasses or crystal. The table glistens, sparkles and looks amazing with nothing else, but a simple vase filled with one type of white flower makes it stunning.

This elegant look with white plates can be set on a rustic, distressed or raw wood table, and looks very unassuming. On a highly polished, dark mahogany table it looks striking and rich. On a glass table, white settings look dramatic and theatrical. Placed on a picnic blanket with plaids and a vase filled with gerber daisies, white settings look playful, casual and fresh. Set on marble or granite, the natural colors are highlighted, and with some clear candleholders, glass, Lucite or crystal, they can be quite a showpiece.

After you have accumulated plates of all sizes for salad, dessert and dinner, build a good collection of serving pieces. A large clear bowl is best for salad because it is beautiful to see through to the greens. A few large platters are necessary for cheese and crackers; turkey and ham; and for big holiday gatherings. I also love to use large platters to carry glasses because that makes it so easy to move them around on the evening of a party.

Make sure you have medium sizes, in bowls and platters, for celebrations of six to eight guests. Bowls are necessary, but since you will use them less, I don't suggest collecting these for daily use. Use them only as serving pieces.

Beautiful flatware also should be in your cabinet. Budget will dictate what kind you can have, but as I've already mentioned, sterling and silver plate can often be found at reasonable prices in antique-type stores. I'd buy the best you can afford, but be diligent and search out great places to buy. I have seen sets for as little as $100, which is great, because they can start out at significantly higher prices.

The Tableware Trousseau

The tableware trousseau holds the items you will reuse for almost every event: vases, votive candleholders, candlesticks, candelabras and centerpieces. I won't include dishes, china or stemware in this category, because those are stored in the china cabinet. This is the cabinet you come to in order to see what you need, and what you already have, when beginning to plan a party.

When organizing or planning your tableware trousseau, utility and reusability is the key. Make sure the pieces you store here can be used an infinite number of times. A few years ago, the prospect of having a filled linen closet or trousseau for parties of up to 12 seemed daunting on a budget, but it doesn't have to be. There are numerous ways to begin a collection, and a combination of the following will probably be your best bet. Keep in mind, especially if you are a younger reader, that your collection won't come together overnight. But the collecting is part of the fun. And

after a year or two, you will find quite a difference in your collection.

The Process

Antiquing. If you like to shop, you'll find this the most fun. Antiques have the charm and character that is often missing from newer pieces, and you can make antiquing an enjoyable outing with a friend or your husband.

You can create beautiful tables by mixing and matching place settings—china, stemware, silver and napkins—with each setting different from the next. Collect as you go. When you are on vacation, bring back something besides a cheap souvenir. A friend may be able to do this for you, or you for them, if you have a specific collection.

Traveling. It is always so interesting when in someone else's home to hear the stories behind their unique purchases. This brings back wacky and wonderful memories and weaves a family's story throughout their home. Once, while driving home from Portugal, we stumbled on an antique dealer's home, where we found a treasure trove of antiques, including pots that were hundreds of years old. We fell in love (okay, a slight exaggeration) with the most wonderful Portuguese hutch, but it was way too big for our car. So, after arriving home in Spain, we convinced some wonderful friends who owned a van to drive four hours back with us to pick up the hutch on another weekend. We had another wonderful weekend in Portugal, with half of the hutch strapped to the top of the van so that our friends' children would fit in the van. The hilarity that ensued while two dentists and one very toothless and tenacious antiques dealer tried to squish a huge armoire into an average size van was quite worth the drive. I very helpfully stood in the background and gave moral support by telling them it would fit.

Searching for specific collections. A teacup collection is fun (if you like to have tea), because there are practically an infinite number of teacups to find. Since each is unique, it is fun to take out your collection and have everybody (including yourself) ooh and ahh over the beautiful patterns and colors.

Once, when we were in Belgium, I almost spent my allotted budget for the day when I spotted an antique shop with the most lovely teacups and linens. They had a basket with mismatched linens for $1 per piece. I selected some that were absolutely beautiful. They looked so lovely once they were washed and ironed. What a fun way to add to my tea collection and get a souvenir at the same time.

Birthday and other special gifts. A great way

to build a collection is through friends and family. I love to buy gifts that I know my friends will enjoy and use, and so does my family. My wonderful in-laws try to find fun things for my plate and serving piece collections; I love buying teacups for my friends who have teacup collections. If I'm spending my hard-earned money, I don't want to give a gift that will end up in a closet, never to be used. I try to make sure they will use and enjoy it!

Trading. My sister and I love to trade accessories and small pieces of furniture. We each know anything that comes from the other will seem like brand new, and we can always get it back if we really miss it. If it is a family piece, then it is still in the family, and it feels great knowing that something so sentimental is still around.

Remember to concentrate on building just a little of your collection at a time, as you will complete it sooner, and be able to use it and lend it out! Collect different things than your close friends and neighbors so that you can trade, have more to use and less to store. ■ ■ ■

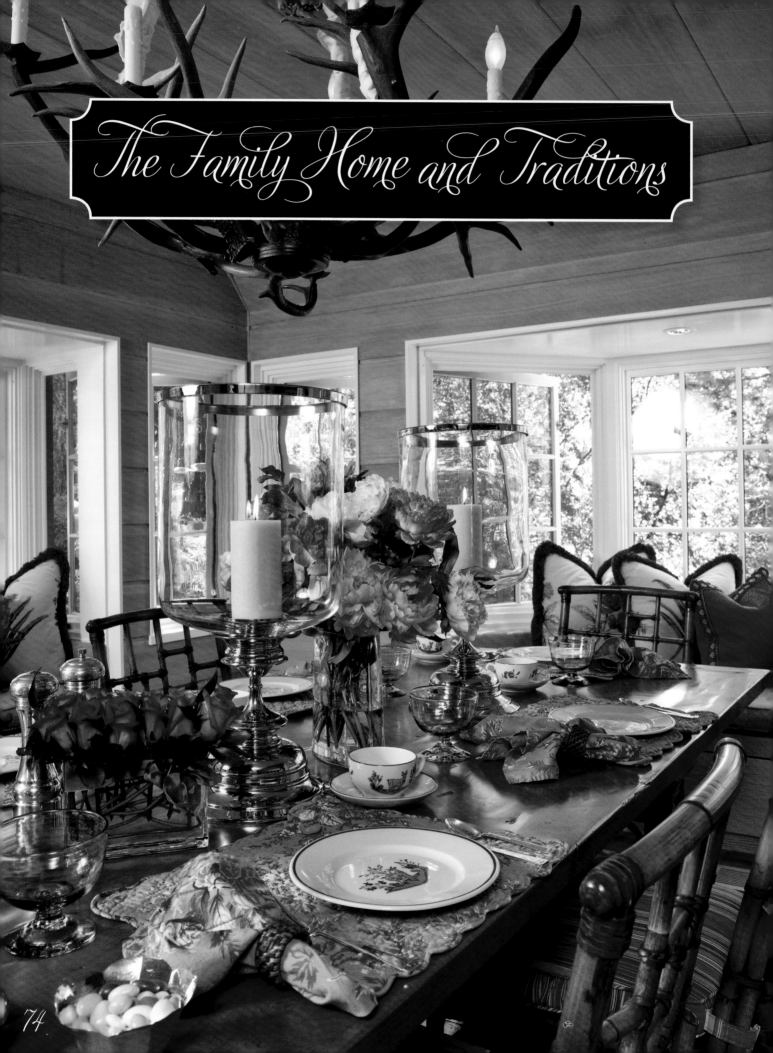

The Family Home and Traditions

The Family Home and Traditions

LEARNING FROM MOM

I am a visual learner, and growing up, I watched my mom get so much joy from making occasions special memories for my sister and me. She has the world's best taste, and she taught me much about design. But what made her exceptional was that she expressed her love by setting a magnificent table.

She prepared spectacular decorations for holidays and left no detail untended. She was a homemaker, and she took pride in making a warm and enchanting home. Even in the early years, when she didn't have much, mom went to great lengths to make sure things were just right. At the time, I didn't have much of an appreciation for the love, time and hard work that it took. Now that I'm a mom, I do.

My favorite family tradition—and Hannah's too—is Rolly Pancakes. We had them for breakfast almost every Sunday morning. It made no difference whether we were on the "Shawnee" (My grandparents' beloved sailboat), at Catalina Island, California, or at our family home in Lake Arrowhead.

Mom would start by making French crepes (Hannah and I love anything French) and a delicious orange sauce. Then she served them with powdered sugar. When mom made Rolly Pancakes for our large family, it usually took two or three hours.

The ornament of a house
is the friends who frequent it.
–Ralph Waldo Emerson

A kind word is like a spring day.

- RUSSIAN PROVERB

78

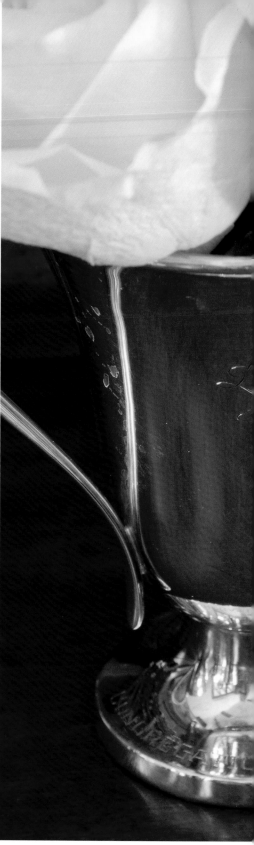

If you have only one smile in you,

give it to the people you love.

– Maya Angelou

Since I am now in charge of this endeavor, I fully appreciate both the little darlings who are sitting at the table, hungrily waiting their turn to eat a crepe, and the cook who is in the kitchen, making between 30 and 50 of them. Both are special memories, and I love them! What's more, I will never forget the laughter and bonding around the table, as the meal was slowly being prepared and served.

Traditions that are uniquely your own create special memories that will be passed down to your children, and theirs. Our traditions revolve around the table, table settings and family memories, as do many of yours I'm sure. Our children look to what we do more than we realize. As we go along in our day, cooking, setting the table, wrapping gifts, lighting candles and getting the guest room ready for company, little eyes are wide open, soaking in instruction. Every act of kindness, and every effort to make something a little nicer for someone else, is something our children will pick up, and learn from.

Rolly Pancakes

Crepes

2 cups flour   2 cups milk
4 eggs   Dash of salt

Sauce

2 cups fresh or frozen orange juice
1/2 cup butter
1 tbsp powdered sugar
1 tsp. Orange Rind (fresh or dried) as desired

PLACE ON TABLE:
Bowl of powdered sugar to sprinkle on crepe, and on the inside if you like it sweeter

ORANGE SAUCE:
Make this first, so while this boils, then simmers, you can make the batter.

DIRECTIONS:
Put all the ingredients into saucepan, bring to just a boil, then reduce heat to simmer, until sauce thickens. I usually allow about 15 minutes, but you just want it thicker than regular orange juice. I always make a bigger batch, then freeze some, and put some in the fridge, since my kids get this most mornings for breakfast! Microwave it, and in two minutes it's ready!

CREPE:
Mix ingredients for crepes with a whisk, making sure the lumps are out of the batter and that it doesn't get too thick. You can add about 1/4 cup of milk if you want them to be thinner. High altitude does affect the proportions, so add more milk as necessary. Use oil not butter in the crepe pan, and fix like a crepe. (Thin, roll the pan so the batter is spread thin, stand right there, flip when bubbles appear) You want it to just turn brown, not really brown like a regular pancake.

No act of kindness, no matter how small, is ever wasted.

—Aesop

God could not be everywhere, so he created mothers.

~ Jewish Prove[rb]

Hannah's
POINT OF VIEW

[I] feel blessed to have the house in Lake [A]rrowhead. I love it because it has been [i]n the family for a while. I appreciate it [b]ecause of the memories I have there, [a]nd also for the memories that my [f]amily has. Just looking at the pictures [t]hat line the wall, I get a glimpse of [e]verything that has happened here [o]ver the years, and it really feels neat.

My memories are mostly just bei[ng] there and relaxing. I also rememb[er] countless laughs that I have had wh[en] on the dock with my friends, and wh[en] in the house with my family. I love h[ow] when the sun comes out I can go do[wn] to the beach and swim. I love that [I] can go outside to sled when it snows[.] know that no matter what the weath[er] I can always come back to a warm co[zy] home. I love walking in the door, ju[st] knowing that now I can relax and forg[et] whatever stresses might have seem[ed] so horrible before.

Hannah

GERONIMO

CHAEL HALE   IT'S A ZOO OUT HERE

NATURALCURIOSITIES

HAVEN & CO.

Quality is not an act. It is a habit.
— Aristotle

Great Grandma

Baby Hannah

Hannah and Roxanne

Dear Family Friends

> *T*hink of all the beauty still left around you and be happy.
>
> — Anne Frank

Canadian Family

Dear Friends

Scott's Family

Baby Allison, Hannah, Charlie, and Daniel

Justin and Daniel

Those who bring sunshine to the lives of others cannot keep it from themselves.
— James Matthew Barrie

Oaks Varsity Pole Vaulters

Family

The Rat Patrol

My Precious Little Family

"Dad"

Baby Hannah and Kendra

Baby Hannah and Roxanne

Family

Best Mammoth Friends

The Pampered Guest— and the Gracious Homemaker

Since you bought this book, you probably love to pamper others. The guest room is the perfect way. The mechanics are important to a degree, but make no mistake: it is the love and warmth you share with your guests that will make the real impression.

Think of being a good host as you would think of being a good friend. It has nothing to do with impressing people, although that can be a result, because people will be so touched by your efforts. What is important is remembering special things—from the big ones to little ones.

During my time at USC, I used to spend the night at Grandma Becca's to get away from the commotion. She never did anything spectacular to prepare, but the special touches she had ready for me still make me warm and fuzzy when I think of them. She'd turn the light on, pull the bed back, stack a blanket at the end and get me a glass of water. She'd place a towel and washcloth in the bathroom I would use, and sweetly ask me if there was anything else I needed! We'd chat by the television, while Grandpa Allan slept on the couch until we woke him up to go to bed. The memories are etched in my heart.

The mechanics of a well-stocked guest room are comfortable

sheets, blankets, towels, a carafe of water, a drinking glass, an alarm clock, a stack of reading material, a reading lamp that can be turned off from the bed and a nightlight. Whether they stay for long or short period of time, your guest room is a wonderful way to show kindness to friends, family and, sometimes, strangers. If you have room for a chair, a little sofa or a chaise, that is even more lovely. A beautiful lamp with soft light, along with fresh flowers or sentimental photographs, also add tranquility to a room that you or your guests will want to retreat to for hours. Soft carpeting is always welcome in a bedroom. If you have hard floors, a rug by the bed is key.

Appropriate covering for windows is essential, whether in a guest room or your own room. Be sure all windows have coverings for privacy, and are room darkening for those trying to sleep in, or who have to work during the night and sleep during the day. A tray for snacks set-up with special treats will really make guests feel welcome.

When staying with some friends in Wenatchee, Washington—yes, that really is a town—my husband and I discovered that our hosts had placed a darling basket in the bathroom with travel-sized shampoo, conditioner, toothpaste, toothbrushes, dental floss, nail polish remover, rubber bands, Q-tips, cotton balls, Kleenex and mouthwash. It was practical, as we did forget a few things, and it was also a very thoughtful gesture.

Beautiful bedspreads, duvet covers and pillows in beautiful fabrics are the keys to decorating any bedroom, and the guest room is no exception. Since the bed is a focal part of the room, make it beautiful and cozy. The room should be restful, soft and a place of retreat.

If at all possible, no work should be done in the bedroom. Whether single or married, your bedroom should be a place of rest and rejuvenation. Comfortable sheets are a must, and I like white best, as white sheets can be bleached. The softer the sheets, the better. Throw pillows are the place to splurge, although I think every male client I have ever had would disagree. It is a universal fact that married men do not share our affinity for beautiful pillows.

I like a washable duvet cover for daily use, and a duvet folded at the end of the bed in a stunning fabric. To me, a bedroom isn't finished until there is a duvet folded over the end of the bed. I prefer not to use silk for the bedding as it is impractical. Cotton is the easiest to care for, and seems to perform best over time. A throw blanket, over a chair or on a bench, is really great in case your guest gets cold, and another pop of color or fabric really adds to the warmth of the room. If there is enough space, place a bench at the end of the bed. It's a great place to lay clothes, or items to put away, and decoratively, it is a great way to finish the furniture scheme. Along with the nightstand and a dresser, I consider this a crucial piece for any bedroom. Lastly, remember to mix fabrics, because this is a warm way to add personality to a room. Depending on your taste, it doesn't need to match, and it will give the room a real flair. ■ ■ ■

"Every day we live is a priceless gift of God

to gain fresh insights into

loaded with possibilities to learn something new,

"His great truths." - Dale Evans

94

Making Special Occasions Un

orgettable

C elebrating and honoring my beloved friends and family is one of my favorite things to do. If I had the time and the money, there would be a party every day to honor someone! There are a million reasons to have a party—birthdays, anniversaries, weddings, baby showers, retirements, promotions, graduations and more. Some ideas you may not have thought of include a Tea Party In Honor Of, a Teenage Blessing Tea, a prayer tea, a thanksgiving lunch to show thanks for your friends, a gratitude lunch for teachers, a cookie exchange, a baking party for kids, a cooking class, a tailgate picnic or a picnic in the backyard.

You could host an "Après-ski" dessert, a beach picnic, a movie night, a "look at the Christmas lights" and dessert, a Fourth of July barbeque and picnic, an advent night, a gingerbread house decorating party, a Super Bowl party, a tree decorating party, a victory over cancer celebration or a bon voyage party. Any reason for a celebration will do. Just remember, the true importance of each celebration is to honor the person.

Oh Boy!

Please join us
for a
Baby Shower
&
Luncheon
honoring
Michele

Saturday, June twentieth
at one o'clock
Camarillo, California

given with love by
Hannah & Roxanne

Aunt Mimi loves elephants and duckies
Baby's room colors are Creme & White
Kindy reply by June 10th
Roxannepackhamdesign@yahoo.com

To do the useful thing, to say the courageous thing, to contemplate the beautiful thing: that is enough for one man's life. — T S Eliot

99

Sweet Baby Charlie

With each flower you cut, every cookie you bake and every setting you place, remember that you are making things beautiful to honor them. If something unexpected happens and every last detail is not taken care of, keep in mind that it's about the person, not the fuss.

There are many nice touches you can include: beautiful invitations, a menu at each place with a quote or scripture, or if you are serving a buffet, cards to indicate what each dish is. Making these cards is a perfect job for the kids. Hang a welcome sign above the front door, or welcome your guests with a cheery message on a chalkboard, together with a favorite scripture. Set out fresh flowers or freshly baked cookies. Your guests will simply love them!

Be a gracious host. Honor others, celebrate their accomplishments and make them feel special. Even small celebrations are important, especially to your children. Never miss a chance to be part of making their day.

I have a red plate that says, "You are special." I set it out whenever one of my kids gets a good grade, a positive comment from a teacher or does something especially kind for another person. They love it, and it adds an extra happy note to a regular dinner. Thoughtful gestures, even small ones, can make a huge difference in others lives. In our world today, they are all too rare.

When your kids come home with a problem, listen to them, help them and then encourage them to focus on their positive traits, the gifts they have been given by God and how they can use them best. This attitude of gratitude is what fills a house with love. ■ ■ ■

Live in harmony with one another; be sympathetic, love as brothers, be compassionate and humble. - 1 Peter 3:8

Andrea

This is the day
that the Lord
has made; we
will rejoice and
be glad in it.
Psalm 118:24

Hannah's
POINT OF VIEW

Mimi's shower was special—not just because of the people who came, but because of the time put into it. My mom and I spent hours getting ready, and it showed in every little detail, from the napkins to the set-up of the presents. Mom put thought and time into the presentation of our home and the way it looked for the people who would be joining us that afternoon. She does this for all of her parties, and it adds to the festiveness of the occasion. To put it simply, you can't just casually go to the store, get some party decorations, put them up in twenty minutes and come up with what my mom came up with. It just isn't possible. Thought is the biggest difference between boring and spectacular.

— Hannah

Whatsoever things are true, honest, just, pure, lovely, of good report, If there be any virtue, if there be any praise, Think on these things.
- Philippians 4:8

105

You cannot do a kindness too soon, fo

you never know how soon it will be too late.
-Ralph Waldo Emerson

Celebrating Friends & Family

"The more you praise and celebrate your life, the more there is in life to celebrate." — Oprah Winfrey

109

~ Southern Charm ~

What woman doesn't love the idea of sitting down with a cup of tea and catching up with a dear friend? Or better yet, going to a teahouse— the Peninsula, Hotel Bel Air or the Beverly Hills Hotel—for a traditional tea? Women everywhere love to entertain and be entertained. But Southern hospitality is in a class by itself—endearing, enchanting and engaging.

My clients, Wendy and Dave, although born and raised in California, spent several years in Georgia. They fell head over heels in love with the South. They loved the beautiful, plantation-style homes, the huge expanses of grass for their four children to play on, the community feel and the big, friendly hearts of the people.

Upon meeting them my directions were simple: to make a beautiful Southern-style home on a budget. Wendy didn't have a lot of time to spend with me. She was home-schooling four children, while building her home. But I loved the project, because she really trusted me!

Once I met Wendy, it didn't take long to discover she is a perky, determined, intelligent homemaker who adores having her kids' friends and their families over. She needed a schoolroom for her home school, and we chose a beautiful dining room table so that when the children were older she could use it as extra seating for parties. Although the property the home is built on is large, the home itself is not huge, so furniture had to be carefully selected and placed. We chose a large, dark mahogany round table for the dining room, and matched it with cream painted and distressed French chairs upholstered with pink and green striped French fabric. Set against dark hardwood floors and kelly green toile drapery, the effect is stunning. This kept the feeling casual yet elegant. The furnishings we chose were also durable, which is important because the kids spend a lot of time in there.

When Wendy and Dave first saw the grey-tinted pastel color of their walls, they almost panicked. But I pleaded with them to wait until the dark hardwood floors were in, along with the drapes and furniture. I promised they would love it, and they did. The moral of the story: wait until the entire project is finished to see the finished look!

Love begins at home, and everyone should try to make sure that deep family love abides in his or her home. Only when love abides at home can we share it with our next-door neighbor. – Mother Teresa

Those who bring sunshine into the lives of others cannot keep it from themselves. — James Matthew Barrie

113

Now Faith is the Substance of Things

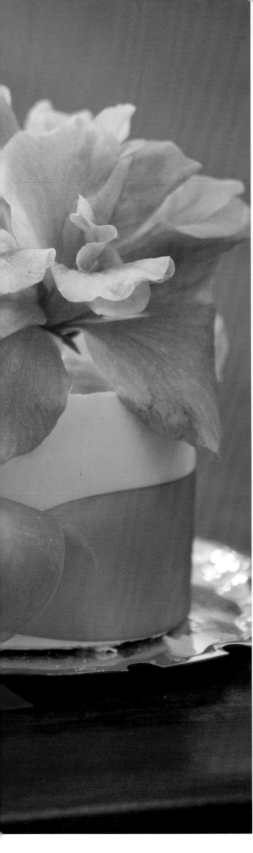

Hoped for, the Evidence of Things not Seen.

Hebrews 11:1

~ The Teenage Blessing Tea ~

The Teenage Blessing Tea idea grew out of what I have seen practiced in different faiths when a child becomes a teenager. In Judaism, for example, there is the Bar or Bat Mitzvah. I made it up as I went, and several friends followed suit, as a way to encourage and bless their daughters.

Because our family is large, we selected 10 to 15 special women who have really meant something to Hannah over her lifetime. No children or friends were invited. We wanted to keep the focus on my daughter, avoid hurt feelings and escape the "just a party" feeling. Hannah's grandmothers and aunts were included, as were a favorite teacher, her godmothers and some other women who are dear to her and me. I let her select the list, because I wanted the women to be women she could go to if something ever happened to me—or if she simply would rather go to them, and not me. I hope that never happens. But if it does, I want her to know whom I think will provide wise counsel.

We chose women who exemplified kindness, integrity and fun! Some were very close friends. We sent out invitations explaining that we wanted to "Bless Hannah" with words of wisdom and affection. I didn't have a formal "scrapbook," but simply requested each write out some words, verses or favorite quotes, and include some sentiment about what made Hannah, my beloved daughter, special. I also requested they bring the oldest photograph they had with her.

We served a traditional tea, and set a traditional tea table. The day was breathtaking, unforgettable. After we feasted on delicious tea and delicacies, I began telling each guest how special she was to Hannah and me. As we went around the table, I would read from a 3x5 card about how each had blessed us, and I would name some particular trait that I wanted Hannah to learn from them.

I expected this to go by quickly, but it became a very sentimental part of the day. There were many tears. Three hours later, when we finished, a chorus of ladies was saying that they each wanted a "blessings tea," and raving about how validating and encouraging it would be. I was amazed at how touched each was to hear that there was something I wanted my daughter to learn from them.

There were warm, sweet and so poignant observations about Hannah and her unique gifts, and they made the day special for Hannah and me. It was exactly what I had hoped it would be, a way to give her all kinds of meaningful encouragement that she would remember as her teenage years progressed. Sometimes high school can get ugly, although so far, so good.

I created an album from the cards, notes and photographs we collected that day. Both of us have savored that notebook and the memories of that tea. As much as it blessed Hannah, it may have been an even greater blessing to the friends and family who were there and heard that their life's example was one I treasured for my daughter. They, too, were honored and uplifted—an added blessing of the Teenage Blessing Tea. ■ ■ ■

Taste and see that the Lord is good.
Psalm 34:8

Hannah's
POINT OF VIEW

My memory of the Blessing Tea is fairly simple. It feels really special to have people tell you that they will always be there for you when you need them. It just encouraged me to be myself, which I realize is very important. It was a really encouraging time, and it made a memory I won't ever forget. The ladies from the tea were so kind and uplifting to me. I will always remember who I am and that I am very loved.

— *Hannah*

High Tea
WITH THE TEA GROUP

119

Creating A Home
That Radiates Happiness

Decorating adds the charm that most houses lack, and turns them from just a house into a home. The memories we have of our home growing up are likely from the warmth (or lack of it) that existed there. My memories of home are a gift!

I grew up in a home where I felt loved, supported and encouraged. I was surrounded by humor, for sure! I hope you also have happy memories of growing up. But even if you don't, you can adopt some of these ideas for your family. That's because a loving home has something to do with design, but it is mostly about good parenting. The memories you are making with your children in your home are memories that will be etched in their minds forever.

It isn't what you have that matters; it's what you do with it.

The first home my husband and I shared was just 500 square feet. It sat on the back lot of someone else's home, on an alley, with no fireplace or other distinctive features. It had little in the way of physical attractiveness, but our home was beautiful, warm and full of love. Even while tripping over the furniture to get to the bathroom, our little "cottage"—that was a generous term for this place—radiated happiness.

The charm infused by decorating, and the warmth of special touches, made all the difference. Even if your home is humble, these can do the same for you. Color can make a cold room, warm and inviting. The best advice I can give you is, be brave.

What makes a color the perfect color for a room is that you love it! Not long after we added on to our house, I decided that since I was sooooo good with color I would paint my new family room a lime green. After it was finished, my mom came to visit and I showed it to her. She and I walked into the lovely room, with its French fireplace and the new neon green, and started laughing so hard we had to sit down to catch our breath. By the time my mom woke up the next morning, I had the room completely repainted.

The families whose rooms are featured in this chapter have eclectic tastes and chose orange as a feature color. Orange is a very warm, embracing color that envelops you without knocking you over. I like to use it sparingly—a solid orange sofa, which might blow you off your feet. But it is a cheerful, vibrant, happy color that is full of life and great for an active family. It also lends itself to contemporary design, and for these young families it was a fun complement to fairly traditional decorating schemes.

Hannah's
POINT OF VIEW

In this home, the colors and patterns look so comforting and inviting. Home should be a comforting place, and colors and patterns have much to do with creating that feeling. Outside colors calm and soothe people. This is why a walk outside feels so nice. It is an inviting environment, and the same principles apply to a home. The more welcoming, comforting and inviting it is, the better. Of course, the most important way you make your home inviting is by taking the time to make others feel welcome, and in the Browder home that is certainly true.

— Hannah

The essence of love is kindness.
- Robert Louis Stevenson

Mixing fabric patterns and colors is one of the best ways to show your taste and personality throughout your home. The more original and eclectic the mix, the better the design will complement you and your tastes. The more bold and colorful the patterns and the mix, the more energetic, playful and relaxed the mood is. The more subtle the colors, and the smaller the pattern, the softer and more elegant the look and feel will be. Patterns are great for active families, because they don't show dirt and wear as much. They also look very playful. Stripes, plaid and florals can be great together—if the colors just sing. ■ ■ ■

Joy is the simplest form of gratitude.

- Karl Barth

Your Home: A Reflection of You

When it reflects the people who live inside, a home just sings. Make sure your passions are represented throughout your home, through collections, art, objects, photographs or a library. Your passion doesn't have to be something you have accomplished; it may be something you love or want to try.

Is your passion collecting great books? They can be displayed in different ways all over the house. You may be passionate about quotations or scriptures. They can be displayed with embroidery on pillows, written above doorwells, painted onto drywall, artfully lettered and framed or lettered over photographs and beautifully displayed on a wall. They can be carved into a mantel or a cabinet, painted onto a tile or wood floor and stained over, written on the backs of staircases or etched around a mirror. The options are almost too numerous to count.

If cooking is your passion, favorite recipes can be framed into a desk frame and placed on shelves in the kitchen. If cycling is your passion, a photograph of you cycling can be framed and displayed on a hallway wall, with cycling paraphanalia or trophies. If you have traveled to participate in or watch cycling events, those, too, can be incorporated. If each family member has a passion, they can have their own spot in the home, perhaps a wall in different hallways, to display their moments.

I'm sure when you think of your own passions, or collections, something pops right into your mind. But you might have a hard time. Just ponder this and keep thinking of what you enjoy: What do I like to watch? Read? Listen to? What do I like to cook or eat? Who do I hang out with?

When decorating an entire room or house around one theme or passion, be careful not to be too obvious. In other words, if you like dogs, don't just fill your house with a jillion items with dogs on them. Use the idea subtly. Use fabrics with dog prints on them. Make things in the shape of a paw print. Incorporate books about dogs throughout the house. Use earth tones to complement the dogs' colors. Fill a glass jar with dog bones, have a Christmas tree with only dogs on it, make lamps out of antique bronze dog statues and use antique dog show awards as bookends. Use "dog" items as the undertone, so that "dog" isn't the focus of the home.

Traveling and Passion

Hannah and I are passionate about Paris! When she was a little girl, her room was a "Pink Paris" room. We both loved that room, with its Eiffel towers, French poodles, toile, French signs, and Hannah's favorite Bible verse, Matthew 7:7, painted, in French, around the room. From the time she was four, I had her tutored in French by my favorite French friend, Pascale. She is just completing French Honors III, so my passion has turned into hers.

Hannah and I took a very special antique-buying trip to Paris, with her dear friend, Imogen, and her mother Francesca. We had a magical time, and the memory will be forever etched in our minds. We combined a fun and productive learning experience and a vacation with dear friends. We made a memory, learned a lesson or two and came home with great stories, wonderful photographs and some fabulous antiques! Many of my clients are enjoying those purchases, which are also included in many of the photographs thoughout the book.

I became passionate about Paris during college, when I attended the Sorbonne, and the Paris Fashion Institute. I love everything French, and I have adopted their love of culture and art. While living there, I grew to appreciate their lifestyle, their love of good, fresh food and their love of design. The French really know how to enjoy all different cultures. While I love being an American, I also adore the French people, their beautiful language and their appreciation for art and the artistic lifestyle.

Wherever you go, whatever you love, whatever you want to learn about—document it! Keep a journal to sketch and write in. Not only is it a special memento, it is a learning tool. Become an expert at what you love.

If you are going somewhere and you love art, go to several art museums. Make the day of it; have lunch there, too. If cost is an issue, buy a few postcards to remind you of the museum and its works of art, instead of the book on the exhibit. If you love to cook, take cooking lessons. If you love to cycle, take a cycling tour of the area. If you love boats, take a boat tour.

A good way to organize your excursion is through the hotel concierge. If you aren't staying in a hotel, and you have an American Express credit card, they have a travel service that is free of charge, and I often use it to do the research for tours. As a card member, you will often get better seats than even the hotel concierge can get you for concerts, the theatre and dinner

Paris is always a good idea. -Audrey Hepburn

reservations. On a vacation, that is the way to go. Professional organizations in the area may be able to answer your questions. You can also Google the name of the city, along with terms like "cooking," "design" and "art," or go to the library or a bookstore. And be sure that you document your trip with photographs. They will make great momentos for you home, especially if you display them in a unique way.

Gifts and Gift Wrapping

The best gift givers are people who pay attention to the little details in others' lives—the ones who listen to what others love or need and know about the collections and passions of the receiver. To be a good gift giver is to be focused on the needs and desires of others, and to be thoughtful enough to carry through. A beautifully wrapped present is a gift in itself, and sometimes, it really is almost too beautiful to open.

My sister Michele, of Michele Hughes Design, is a wonderful gift giver and turns wrapping into an art form. She collects wrapping paper, ribbons, little package toppers and cards throughout the year, and stores them in the most organized little wrapping closet you have ever seen. I can spend hours at her house, just looking through her wrapping closet. You can see from the packages pictured here that she is quite talented.

Michele is also a talented interior designer. Her work has appeared in Better Homes and Gardens, California Homes, Valley Magazine, Decorator Showhouses, ASID Kitchen and Interiors Tour, Pasadena Showcase House of Design and Home Wizards. She has decorated homes from Newport Beach, to Pasadena, to Lake Arrowhead, and it is her beautiful work that is featured in this section.

The old saying, "It's the thought that counts," is still true today. It isn't the size or the expense of the gift that matters, but the thought that goes into it. To remember, let alone to hear the desire or need of a friend, then translate it into a thoughtfully purchased gift, can be priceless. To know your friend has a teacup collection, and be thoughtful enough to purchase one in Paris, is a thoughtful and generous gift that is certain to touch the receiver.

Ease the stress of gift giving by having some unique gifts and cards ready to go for a variety of occasions. For a gift wrapping station, choose a room or drawer, whichever you have room for. Make sure it is well stocked—that's crucial to relaxed gift giving. I keep my gift wrapping station right by the back door, because undoubtedly, we are running out the door just as I am trying to tie the bow on a package. When I have more time, I take gifts into our library and spread out on the big table.

When collecting wrapping supplies, remember that it is the unusual that makes a great giftwrap. Instead of using wrapping paper, use a newspaper, a road map, a nautical map, shipping paper, old wallpaper or fabric swatches. School paper may fit the bill for a graduation gift; for an avid golfer, use pages from a golf magazine. Use a coordinating ribbon or something black or white, to keep some consistency.

For package toppers use something original—a pencil for a student, a toothbrush for a child with new braces, a tennis ball cut in half for a tennis player or sand dots (glue dots with sand sprinkled on them) for someone who loves the beach. For an accountant, stick adhesive numbers all over the wrapper. For a polka-dot lover, stick dots all over it For an artist, tie on a paintbrush. You'll think of something that fits the receiver.

A gift doesn't have to be a present. It can be a thoughtful gesture, like a rose on a bad day. It can be a hot cup of tea, or a picnic for a friend who is struggling with anxiety. Few gifts are better than homemade chicken soup for a sick friend, a basketful of goodies after surgery, or something funny for someone who is depressed and needs to laugh or smile.

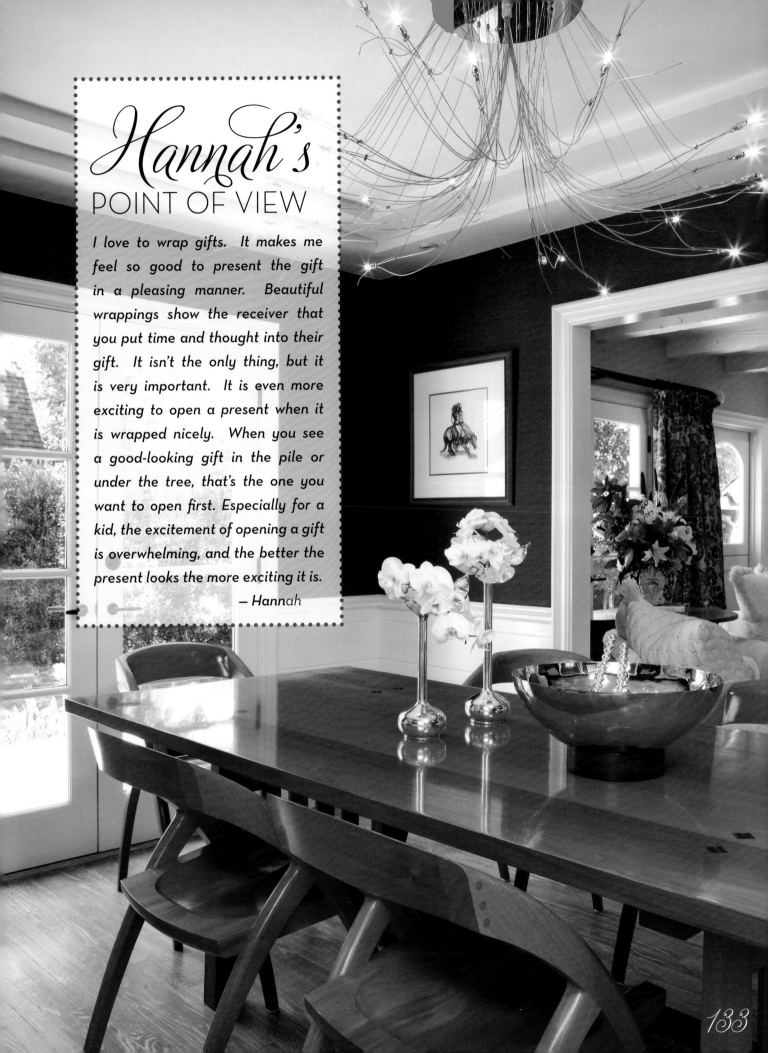

Hannah's
POINT OF VIEW

I love to wrap gifts. It makes me feel so good to present the gift in a pleasing manner. Beautiful wrappings show the receiver that you put time and thought into their gift. It isn't the only thing, but it is very important. It is even more exciting to open a present when it is wrapped nicely. When you see a good-looking gift in the pile or under the tree, that's the one you want to open first. Especially for a kid, the excitement of opening a gift is overwhelming, and the better the present looks the more exciting it is.

— Hannah

133

A Thankful Spirit:
The "Inspired" in Inspired Design

hankfulness and gratitude are key components of inspired design.

I am profoundly grateful for my philanthropic, often hysterically funny husband; my lovely and stylish daughter; my artistic and athletic son; my devoted parents; my dear and treasured friends; a life mission that I love; and a relationship with my Creator that makes my heart overflow.

If we didn't have friends in our home, and if it wasn't filled with the joy that friendship brings, it wouldn't feel "inspired." Take my dear friend, Courtney, whom I have known since my freshman year at USC. She picked me to be her little sis in our sorority, which was the biggest blessing! She is an amazing person: talented, intelligent, sensitive and very intuitive. Our friendship is over 25 years old! We have weathered and celebrated boyfriends, weddings, marriage, children, lousy friends, mean people, death, family tragedies and living on different continents. Her friendship is such a gift. Each of us celebrates the other's accomplishments and takes part in the fun. She was a bridesmaid in my wedding, and I was in hers.

Of the bridesmaids in my wedding, I still keep in touch with all but one (she moved away and I lost touch!) and speak to them quite frequently. They are my dear friends—Lori, Sandy, Sally, Stacey, Kerry, Andrea, Corinne, Courtney, and my sister, Michele—and the best blessings I have! Another special group is my Tea Club Group: Lorianne, Joy, Nancy, Deana, Kathleen and Camille. We met as new mothers and have shared the joys of raising children together. They are truly a part of who I am, and have become.

I do not take friendship lightly. I treasure being loved unconditionally, and think our greatest purpose on earth is to love one another, as Christ loved us. Our home is filled with friendships and relationships; what is important to our family is to be loving and inclusive. The example of loving crosses all barriers, and all faiths.

Where there is gratitude, joy overflows. It is hard to let complaining or feeling sorry for yourself ever creep in. If we can focus on what is going right, it is easier to handle the difficult parts of life. Gratitude also allows you to help others handle the tough stuff.

Christ's example was one of love and inclusion, not criticism and exclusivity. Follow it. When Jesus Christ came down to earth, it was no happenstance that He was born in a barn and lived among the regular people, or that He chose average people with flaws as his disciples. We can take from this that God wants us to be kind, and to welcome other people into our homes and our lives.

Kindness is the best way to show Christ's love. No matter what you achieve, no matter what you say, what you actually do—the love and kindness you show others—will be your legacy. ■ ■ ■

The most I can do for my friend is simply to
If he knows that I am happy in loving him, he

e his friend. I have no wealth to bestow on him.

will want no other reward. — *Henry David Thoreau*

Hannah's
POINT OF VIEW

I am thankful that I have such wonderful friends surrounding me. I am blessed to have many people to laugh and share memories with. It truly is a blessing. I also am so thankful for health—both mine and that of my family. And one more very important thing: I am blessed to have a great family. I find it very comforting to have such a loving and encouraging family that supports me in what I do.

— Hannah

I awoke this morning with devout thanksgiving for

my friends, the old and the new. -Ralph Waldo Emerson

Our Beautiful & Dear Friends

The beauty of a woman is not in the clothes she wears, the figure that she carries, or the way she combs her hair. The beauty of a woman is seen in her eyes, because that is the doorway to her heart, the place where love resides. True beauty in a woman is reflected in her soul. It's the caring that she lovingly gives, the passion that she shows & the beauty of a woman only grows with passing years. ~"
— Sam Levinson, spoken by Audrey Hepburn

143

Christmas Decorations and Traditions

Let Him have all your worries and cares, for He's always thinking about you and watching everything that concerns you.
1 Peter 5:7

*I*n my mind, I've turned the clock back 30 years. My sister and I are all dressed up in matching plaid dresses. We're getting ready for Christmas Eve dinner, and posing for pictures in front of the brick fireplace in our first house. I am old enough to remember how excited we were that Santa Claus would come and leave presents. I remember how much fun it was to have our crazy, loud family all together for Christmas.

I have so many fond memories of Christmases past, but beautifully set tables, brightly decorated trees and festively wrapped presents are the forefront of my memories. Our family was so much fun, and there was always so much laughter. At Christmas, our home was filled with hysterical storytelling, great food and an appreciation for the blessing of family.

For me, Christmas brings to mind times with family and friends, surrounded with delights for all the senses. In our home, we have always celebrated the original meaning of Christmas, which is the birth of Christ. It is a special time of gratitude. We read the Christmas story from the Bible and share with each other what we are grateful for in our lives. We speak of the blessings that we have been given, in the form of family, friends and things we have taken part of.

Gifts are a fun part of Christmas, and we enjoy the process of wrapping and putting them under the tree for the kids. But we also remember that Christmas represents the ultimate gift, the birth of the Savior Jesus Christ. Christmas brings me back to the reason for Inspired Design, to make people feel loved, included and to set the stage for memories to be made. It's about relationships, relationships, relationships—a relationship with our Creator, relationships with our family, and relationships with friends. It's about loving them, for love is truly inspired.

Just as we began the book with where we came from, we finish the book with where we are going from here. I hope you are inspired to design. Sometimes you may have no idea of how special you have made someone feel, or of the difference you made with a simple invitation. It is often surprising who is actually the most in need. Allow yourself to be surprised. ■ ■ ■

Riches, both material and spiritual, can choke you if you do not use them fairly. For not even God can put anything in a heart that is already full. – Mother Teresa

147

Hannah's
POINT OF VIEW

It feels lovely to sit down at a beautiful table. When I look back at sitting at the Thanksgiving or Christmas dinner table, each looked clean and creative. Honestly that makes each dinner even better. Memories are all I have left of past Christmases and it really makes the memory even better to picture a beautiful setting. I remember all my family events looked wonderful and it contributes to the way I remember all celebrations.

— Hannah

BOUGIE DÉ PARIS

FRANCE

NOEL

You will find as you look back upon your life that the moments when you have really lived are the moments when you have done things in the spirit of love.

- Henry Drummond

SINCERE THANKS TO OUR TEAM:

Mark Lohman
for the beautiful photographs

~

Frank Boross
for endless hours of excellent layout and design

~

Elizabeth Lessert
for her editing skills

~

Judy Samsky
for her friendship & managing Roxanne Packham Design, Inc.

Special Thanks to:

Chuck & Lorianne Merritt
of White Post Media
*who so freely gave numerous hours of guidance
to help us so expertly with our mission*

~

Our Amazing Family
(Scott, Justin, Mom and Dad)
*who collectively gave hours of reading,
proofing, bouncing ideas and putting up with "the book"
because they understood the mission!*

~

And most importantly, thanks be to God,
from where our "Inspiration", for Inspired Design came.

With Love,

Roxanne and Hannah